Who Is Lin-Manuel Miranda?

by Elijah Rey-David Matos

illustrated by David Malan

Penguin Workshop

To my God, my family, and my people.
I pray I make you all proud—ERDM

To Penny, for being music
to those around you—DM

PENGUIN WORKSHOP
An imprint of Penguin Random House LLC, New York

First published in the United States of America by Penguin Workshop,
an imprint of Penguin Random House LLC, New York, 2024

Visit us online at penguinrandomhouse.com.

Library of Congress Cataloging-in-Publication Data is available.

Printed in the United States of America

ISBN 9780593750773 (paperback)   10 9 8 7 6 5 4 3 2 1 CJKW
ISBN 9780593750780 (library binding)   10 9 8 7 6 5 4 3 2 1 CJKW

Contents

Who Is Lin-Manuel Miranda?

Lin-Manuel Miranda prepared for his elementary school's piano recital for weeks, and tonight was the night. He'd settled on a song, practiced constantly, and mastered it. Now, with his dad in the crowd, seven-year-old Lin moved onto the duet bench, placed his hands on the keys, and played.

Before he knew it, he finished the song and the audience erupted. He did it! Lin-Manuel loved hearing their applause. He didn't want it to end.

"I know another one!"

Why stop when everyone was having a good time? Lin-Manuel, who friends called "Lin," loved seeing the crowd smile. So, he played another. They were clapping again, maybe even louder this time. He played four more songs! Every time Lin finished one the audience clapped, but, eventually, his teacher led him offstage. Lin knew other kids deserved to have the same fun he did, so he agreed to step away. That night, Lin became a performer. He loved entertaining people, and he planned to keep doing it for many years.

A few years after the recital, Lin's mom saw his talent in a Christmas performance alongside his church choir. She knew there were other kids singing, but in her mind, Lin had the spotlight. After talking it over, the Mirandas committed to

supporting Lin's artistic passions. Lin's dad still hoped he would choose a stable career, like being a lawyer, but his mom was a little more open to Lin's creativity. Thanks to their support and his own hard work, Lin would one day be a global superstar. But before he made it to the stage, he was just another talented Puerto Rican kid from New York City.

CHAPTER 1
The Unsinkable Lin-Manuel

Lin-Manuel Miranda was born on January 16, 1980, to Luis A. Miranda Jr. and Dr. Luz Towns-Miranda. Luis had been born in Vega Alta, a small town in Puerto Rico, but came to New York City to study at New York University, where he met Luz Towns. Luz had been born in Puerto Rico but had moved to New York, just like Luis had. After they met, Luz became a doctor—a clinical psychologist who works with people to improve their mental health. Luis worked with New York politicians including Mayor David Dinkins and Senator Hillary Clinton. At the time Luz and Luis met, Luz already had a daughter who was also named Luz, but who they called "Lucecita." Luis and Lucecita bonded quickly.

Luz Towns-Miranda and Luis A. Miranda Jr.

In 1979, just a few months after Luis and Dr. Luz started dating, they got married! Two months later, Luis adopted Lucecita. Lin was born the following year.

Luis took Lin's name from a poem called "nana roja para mi hijo Lin-Manuel" ("red lullaby for

my son Lin-Manuel"),
written by a Puerto
Rican poet named José
Manuel Torres Santiago.
The poem reflects on the
future of Puerto Rico at
the time of the Vietnam
War and is addressed to
the speaker's son, named
Lin-Manuel.

José Manuel Torres Santiago

Lin grew up listening to all kinds of music. In Puerto Rico, his father had seen a movie adaptation of a musical he loved called *The Unsinkable Molly Brown*.

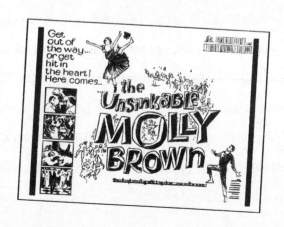

Puerto Rico or "Boriken"

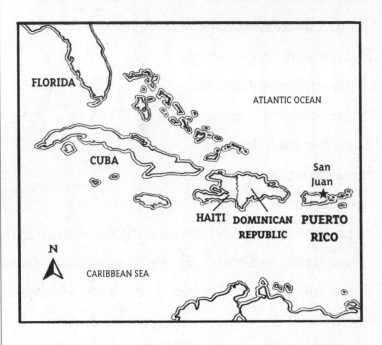

Puerto Rico is a Caribbean island about a thousand miles southeast of Miami, Florida, and is near Cuba, Haiti, and the Dominican Republic. The name "Puerto Rico" means "rich port" in Spanish and was given to the island by the Spanish who arrived to take it over. Before the Spanish took control of

Puerto Rico, the island was called "Boriken" by one group of its Native peoples, the Tainos.

After the 1898 Spanish-American War, Spain ceded the island of Puerto Rico to the United States along with the Philippines and Guam. Today, Puerto Rico is a territory of the United States, and all Puerto Ricans are American citizens. But many Puerto Ricans feel that the United States has treated Puerto Rican residents unfairly. Puerto Rico has no representatives in Congress, and residents of the island cannot vote in general US presidential elections.

Puerto Rico's political parties typically organize around the relationship the island *should* have with the United States going forward. The options for this relationship have usually included Puerto Rico becoming a state, separating as an independent nation, or keeping its status as a territory.

A musical is a live performance in which characters use spoken dialogue, music, songs, and dances to tell a story. When Luis became a father, he made his family watch the movie musical with him all the time, instilling a love for the theater in Lin. Unfortunately, the Mirandas

couldn't afford to attend live shows in Broadway theaters very often. "Broadway" is the general name given to New York City's main area for theaters. Within the Broadway district, there are dozens of professional theaters where musicals and plays are produced at the highest level.

Other, smaller shows in New York are typically referred to as "off-Broadway." If a show gains enough attention from audiences, it will likely move from a smaller off-Broadway theater to one of the larger Broadway ones. Instead of attending these larger and often more expensive performances, the Mirandas listened to a lot of Broadway cast albums, which are recordings of all the songs performed in a musical theater production.

At age seven, Lin finally saw his first

Broadway play named *Les Misérables*. The show is a story about injustices faced by poor and working-class people in France. In his home of Inwood, way up in the northern end of Manhattan, Lin was surrounded by similar New Yorkers who were trying to improve their family's lives. Those families became some of his biggest influences, and their strength shined through in his later projects.

Sometimes young Lin expressed his love for New York in dramatic ways. When his parents sent him to a sleepaway camp at age ten, he wrote letters complaining to his parents about

being unhappy and wanting to come home. Before he went to camp, Lin spent a lot of time inside watching TV, so his parents wanted him to enjoy a summer with other kids. He did make some good friends, but Lin loved his city and couldn't bear to leave it for too long.

During Lin's childhood, his interest in musical theater grew. While he was at Hunter College's middle and high school from 1991 to 1998, he performed in several plays while still finding time to write his own. Off the stage, Lin was listening to a lot of hip-hop and R&B, which his school bus driver and sister played for him. He also carried a boom box throughout Hunter College high school, becoming known for his high-energy personality. He was always ready to put on a show! Some of the first hip-hop artists who influenced him were the Beastie Boys, Rakim, and the Sugarhill Gang.

New York City Hip-Hop

The Bronx, New York, is considered the birthplace of hip-hop. On August 11, 1973, Clive Campbell, known as DJ Kool Herc, and his sister Cindy Campbell hosted a back-to-school party in a recreation room at 1520 Sedgwick Avenue.

DJ Kool Herc

There, Herc's friend, Coke La Rock, shouted attendees' names while Herc played short snippets of live albums from artists like James Brown. Herc's act went on to become famous around the Bronx and helped create a new style of music. Hip-hop culture came to include DJ'ing on the turntables, MC'ing at the mic, breakdancing, and graffiti.

While hip-hop has grown into a global sensation, many of the most beloved rappers and rap groups of all time are connected to New York City's five boroughs. Some of the most notable include Grandmaster Flash and the Furious Five, the Notorious B.I.G., Jay-Z, Nas, the Wu-Tang Clan, A Tribe Called Quest, Slick Rick, Nicki Minaj, Mos Def, Big Pun, Fat Joe, Salt-N-Pepa, and Public Enemy.

As he grew up, Lin found ways to bring together the working-class challenges, hip-hop sounds, and musical theater performances that inspired  him. One of his most important influences was Jonathan Larson's *Rent*, a musical that used rock music and featured young New York artists struggling in the East Village while many of their friends were suffering from the AIDS epidemic, a deadly virus first reported in 1981.

Rent helped push modern rock music into theater alongside a few other shows. Lin saw *Rent* when he was seventeen and was inspired by Jonathan Larson's innovation. As he became more serious about theater, like Larson, he looked to bring the music that he grew up listening to into his work.

Jonathan Larson (1960–1996)

Jonathan Larson was an American composer who was born in New York. He is best known for writing the 1994 musical *Rent,* which put modern rock music at the center of the story. The show became a hit among theater lovers, winning a Pulitzer Prize and four Tony Awards. Unfortunately, Larson would never see the success of the show.

Jonathan Larson

He died the night before previews began off-Broadway at the New York Theater Workshop. While developing *Rent*, Larson lived similarly to the struggling characters in his show, having quit his job at a diner before the play opened. Today, *Rent* and Larson's other musical *tick, tick . . . Boom!* are two of the most acclaimed shows in modern theater.

CHAPTER 2
On to New Heights

From 1998 to 2002, Lin attended Wesleyan University in Middletown, Connecticut, where he studied theater. As a sophomore, he began developing the idea for his first big show.

Wesleyan University

In the Heights tells the story of Dominican bodega owner Usnavi de la Vega, who struggles alongside his neighbors amid the gentrification of his barrio (neighborhood), Washington Heights. Gentrification is a process where people who have more access to resources than those already living in a neighborhood move in and rent or buy property, making it more valuable by paying higher prices for it. Because the new people have extra resources, landlords tend to increase housing prices even more. Those higher prices can be too expensive for the original residents, who are often from BIPOC (Black, Indigenous, People of Color) communities.

Lin's home of Inwood is just north of Washington Heights, so he grew up interacting with members of that barrio. Washington Heights has been dominated by its Latine population for several decades.

With *In the Heights*, Lin wanted to celebrate

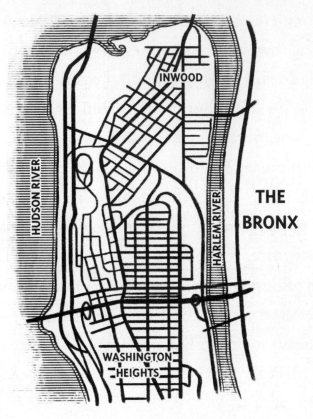

and honor all Latines, especially the ones who live in New York City. In one song, called "Carnaval Del Barrio" (carnival of the neighborhood), performers throw a party in intense heat, encouraging one another to raise up their flags, sing, and dance. Lin filled *In the Heights* with the hip-hop and Latin rhythms that he grew up on, taking inspiration from *Rent*'s use of rock. *In the Heights* also used plenty of "Spanglish," a language that is a mixed version of Spanish and English.

Hispanic or Latino/a/e/ . . . x?

Oftentimes, the labels "Hispanic" and "Latino/ Latina/Latine/Latinx" are used interchangeably. However, there is a difference. "Hispanic" applies to regions that are home to those who primarily speak Spanish. This includes Spain, Puerto Rico, Cuba, and the Dominican Republic and continental American nations like Mexico, Colombia, Peru, El Salvador, Chile, and Honduras. "Latino/a/e/x" applies to people descended from the Americas (including the Caribbean) who speak Spanish, French, or Portuguese. People descended from nations in the Americas where Spanish is the primary language can be considered both Hispanic and Latino/a/ e/x. This means that although Spaniards are not considered Latino/a/e/x, Brazilians, who primarily speak Portuguese, and Haitians, who primarily speak Creole or French, are!

"Latino/a/e/x" has many variations because Spanish, Portuguese, and French are gendered languages. In Spanish and Portuguese, this usually means that "masculine" words, such as *primo* (male cousin) end in "-o" and "feminine" words like *prima* (female cousin) end in "-a." Plural words for groups typically use the masculine ending, such as *primos* or "Latinos"—which are how people from that ethnic group have typically been referenced. "Latinx" and "Latine" have emerged as alternatives to provide a gender-neutral ending for plural words and include people who do not identify as male or female. These terms are considered okay to use no matter your gender.

This book uses "Latine(s)" or "Hispanic-Latine(s)."

In the Heights was first staged by the Second
Stage theater company at Wesleyan University
in 2000. While working on the show, some of
Lin's grades slipped because of his dedication to
the play. Technically, he should've been studying
the universe in his astronomy class, but he was so
focused on *In the Heights* that he wrote some of it
during class. He may not have learned a lot about
the stars in the sky but *In the Heights* would help
him burn just as bright.

After graduating in 2002, Lin returned to Hunter College High School to teach English while advising the school's theater department. Although he loved teaching, Lin believed in *In the Heights*'s potential, and after getting advice from his dad, decided to focus on getting the show produced. Thankfully, his friend Thomas Kail offered to direct *In the Heights* once the show left Second Stage at Wesleyan. At twenty-two years old, Lin had fully committed to following his dreams.

Lin-Manuel Miranda and Thomas Kail

In addition to Thomas Kail, Lin was supported by Jeffrey Seller, a Broadway producer who had worked on *Rent*, Cuban American music director Alex Lacamoire, and Quiara Alegría Hudes, who cowrote with Lin throughout the revision process. Quiara had graduated from both Yale and Brown

Quiara Alegría Hudes

Universities. She is half Jewish and half Puerto Rican, and grew up in Philadelphia. She related to *In the Heights*'s portrayal of urban Latines since she had grown up alongside her mom's Puerto Rican family. Together, Lin and Quiara went through dozens of versions of the play.

While holding rehearsals in the Drama Book Shop's basement for *In the Heights* in 2003 and 2004, Lin, Anthony Veneziale, Thomas Kail, and

In the Heights cast member Christopher Jackson began freestyle rapping about their time on the show. One day, Veneziale suggested they take their act public, and the crew decided to perform as a group called "Freestyle Love Supreme." The day before their opening at the Peoples Improv Theater (PIT) in 2003, a blackout struck the Northeast, including New York City. On the day of the show, the PIT was still without power, so Freestyle Love Supreme walked their audience ten blocks to the Drama Bookshop on Thirty-Ninth Street where electricity had returned and performed the show there.

Freestyle Love Supreme

In 2005, Lin joined a Facebook group for Hunter College high school graduates where he reconnected with Vanessa Nadal, a girl he had known in high school. Vanessa had gone to the Massachusetts Institute of Technology for her bachelor's degree in chemical engineering. When Lin reached out to her, she was working as a development scientist for skincare products. On Facebook, Vanessa noted hip-hop and salsa music as two of her interests. Since their show included freestyle raps, Lin thought it would be a good idea to invite her to a Freestyle Love Supreme performance.

Just like in high school, Lin thought Vanessa was beautiful, but felt so shy he barely spoke to her that evening. After a few nights out with Freestyle Love Supreme and more time talking, the two began dating.

In the Heights opened off-Broadway at the 37 Arts Theatre, now called the Baryshnikov Arts Center, in New York City on February 8, 2007. The original cast included Lin starring as Usnavi, Karen Olivo as Vanessa, Mandy Gonzalez as Nina, and Christopher Jackson as Benny. Eliseo Roman played the *piragüero*, or "piragua guy."

Piraguas

Piraguas are a common dessert throughout Puerto Rico that have been brought to the United States mainland. The treat is shaved ice topped with various syrups that can be mixed according to the customer's request. Piraguas are shaped like a cone and served in a plastic cup with a straw so that customers can sip the mixture of syrup and melted ice. Some typical piragua flavors include *cereza* (cherry), *crema* (cream), *coco* (coconut), *tamarindo* (tamarind), *piña* (pineapple), and *fresa* (strawberry).

Other Latines make desserts like the Puerto Rican piragua. Dominicans often refer to them as *frio frio* (cold cold), Cubans use the term *granizado*, and Mexicans use either *raspa* (scratch) or *raspado* (scraped off).

In the Heights received positive reviews in its debut but was not an instant hit. Luis Miranda stepped in to help his son promote the play, using contacts from his own career to spread the word. By July 2007, *In the Heights* completed its off-Broadway run. While the show was on a break, Lin went on vacation, bringing a very big book with him: Ron Chernow's biography *Alexander Hamilton*, about one of the United States' founding fathers.

After his vacation, Lin made a few adjustments to *In the Heights*. It began Broadway previews on February 14, 2008, at the Richard Rodgers Theatre. On March 9 of that year, the show officially opened to Broadway audiences and

became a hit, earning thirteen Tony nominations and winning four. When Lin claimed the award for Best Original Score (the new music written for the show), he launched into a freestyle rap for his thank-you speech, acknowledging his collaborators, producers, the play's cast and crew, Luis, Dr. Luz, Lucecita, and Vanessa. He ended the speech with the proclamation, "I wanna thank all my Latino people, this is for Abuelo Güisin and Puerto Rico," pulling a Puerto Rican flag out of his suit pocket.

On February 15, 2009, a year after *In the Heights*'s Broadway opening, Lin stepped down from the role of Usnavi. That year, the show was nominated for the Pulitzer Prize for Drama but fell short of winning. Nevertheless, Lin received another honor, being invited to the White House on May 12, 2009, for the Obama administration's inaugural Evening of Poetry, Music, and the Spoken Word. Lin had plenty of songs from *In the*

Heights he could have performed, but, by then, he had begun writing something new.

The Hamilton Mixtape was Lin's idea of a hip-hop concept album that would adapt Ron Chernow's book, telling Alexander Hamilton's story through rap music. A concept album is a collection of music with a complete story connecting each song. As Lin explained, Alexander Hamilton's life followed an unlikely rise to greatness from pain that is often reflected in hip-hop music. Hamilton was born on the island of Nevis but was raised in St. Croix. When he was young, his father left him and his mother. A few years later, Hamilton's mother died, leaving him with little support. After a hurricane struck St. Croix, Hamilton had a letter to his father published in a local newspaper. After reading the letter and seeing Hamilton's skill, a group of businessmen funded his journey to the thirteen colonies, which would lead him to New York.

The New (York) Puerto Ricans

In the 1960s, '70s, and '80s, Puerto Rican residents of New York City founded the Nuyorican movement. "Nuyorican" was originally an insult that separated Puerto Ricans on the island from those born in New York. The founders of the movement changed the meaning of the term to describe their identity as "in-between" New York and Puerto Rico. The Nuyorican tradition focuses on activism, identity, and raising awareness for the struggles of oppressed people on the United States mainland and in Puerto Rico. Oftentimes, Nuyorican artists use spoken word poetry to express these themes. The crowning achievement of the movement was the creation of the Nuyorican Poets Cafe in the Lower East Side neighborhood of Manhattan, or "Loisaida," as it was known among Nuyoricans. Some of the key members of the early Nuyorican movement include Miguel Algárin, Pedro Pietri, Sandra María Esteves, and Ntozake Shange.

Today, the Nuyorican Poets Cafe continues to hold open mic events and has hosted slam poetry champions. Modern Nuyorican poets include "La Bruja" Caridad De La Luz, María "Mariposa" Fernández, and Elisabet Velasquez.

Hamilton's background as an immigrant orphan from the Caribbean who moves to New York resonated with Lin, whose parents had left their Caribbean birthplace in Puerto Rico for New York City, facing discrimination along the way. Hamilton's nonstop work ethic reminded Lin of his dad, who was constantly working when Lin was young. Once again, the Tony Award winner was trying to mix various elements of different cultures in a tribute to his childhood. The tough part was convincing audiences that *The Hamilton Mixtape* could succeed.

Alexander Hamilton

At the White House, Lin rapped the opening song of the project, "Alexander Hamilton," while Alex Lacamoire played the piano. The two introduced the audience to Hamilton as "The ten-dollar founding father without a father" who "got a lot farther by working a lot harder." By the end of the performance, the audience, including President and First Lady Obama, burst into applause. Lin was not yet thirty years old, and he had already received multiple Tony Awards and performed in front of the president and first lady of the United States!

CHAPTER 3
America Then, Told by America Now

On September 5, 2010, Lin and Vanessa Nadal got married in Staatsburg, New York. The legendary Panamanian singer Rubén Blades,

in addition to several Broadway performers, sang at their wedding. In the years that followed, Lin continued working on other shows while developing *The Hamilton Mixtape*.

Lin eventually cowrote the music and lyrics for a stage adaptation of the 2000 film *Bring It On*. The musical centered on a group of teenagers at Jackson High School, led by the character Campbell Davis, who go from being dancers to becoming a cheerleading squad. *Bring It On:*

Bring It On: The Musical

The Musical went on a national tour between 2011 and 2012 with a brief run on Broadway. The adaptation received two Tony nominations for Best Musical and Best Choreography.

As *Bring It On* was on its US national tour,

Lin continued working on the show that he still called *The Hamilton Mixtape*. In the summer of 2013, he began changing *The Hamilton Mixtape* from a concept album to a full musical production. But, since that transition wasn't originally his plan, Lin and his team had a tough time figuring out how to stage and present the show. They were still making edits thirty minutes before his cast had to learn the songs! Chernow's Hamilton biography may have been Lin's vacation read, but *The Hamilton Mixtape* was on its way to becoming a new American revolution.

In March 2014, Lin became even busier. First, he signed on to cowrite songs for an animated Disney movie entitled *Moana*. The film had been inspired by Polynesian myth and features a teenage girl from the Pacific Islands who is called to adventure by the oceans but warned by her family of the danger outside their island.

Moana's family tells her that she is meant to be the chieftain of her island, but she's committed to exploring the world beyond the reef and the safety of her home. Moana leaves the island to fulfill her mission alongside the demigod Maui.

The same day that Lin agreed to work on the

Disney film, he learned that he and Vanessa were going to have their first child. Only a few months into 2014, Lin was adjusting *The Hamilton Mixtape* production, writing lyrics for a Disney movie, and preparing for the birth of his son. Talk about a busy year!

By May 2014, *The Hamilton Mixtape* had transformed into being called simply *Hamilton* and was being staged in New York City at the 52nd Street Project after undergoing workshops at the Public Theater. In the world of musical theater, a workshop is a performance where performers get to show the work they've accomplished, even if it's not yet complete. The workshop is meant to provide audiences a look at the show in a much simpler form. Only a few hundred people got to see this version of *Hamilton*, but it was already gaining momentum as people buzzed about what they had seen. A few weeks after these first performances, Lin put on a short play at the Brooklyn Academy of Music called *21 Chump Street* and costarred in a brief revival of Jonathan Larson's *tick, tick . . . Boom!* In a full-circle moment, Lin portrayed Jonathan Larson, the playwright who had inspired him earlier in his career.

A performance of *tick, tick . . . Boom!*

The end of 2014 brought one last high point to Lin. On November 10, he and Vanessa welcomed their first son, Sebastian Miranda, a moment Lin celebrated with a Twitter post. At the end of the tweet, he wrote "End Of Act One," suggesting the next part of his life was about to start. Between the birth of his first child and *Hamilton* opening off-Broadway at the start of 2015, he couldn't have been more right.

Hamilton opened at the Public Theater on February 17, 2015, when Lin was thirty-five years old. The show was praised for making the United States' early history relatable through modern music and a cast led by BIPOC actors. Many people, including Lin himself, consider the show his masterpiece. However, some critics argued

that casting BIPOC people as the Founding Fathers hid the abuse faced by enslaved Black and Native American people during the country's early days. Others pointed out that women didn't have strong representation, as all the lead roles played by women were romantically interested in Lin's character, Alexander Hamilton.

This criticism aside, *Hamilton* was a smash hit! It became so popular that its transition to the Richard Rodgers Theatre included a lottery system called "Ham4Ham." They called these performances Ham4Ham, or "Hamilton for *Hamilton*," because the show's main character, Alexander Hamilton, is the portrait on the US ten-dollar bill. Since the lottery tickets were only ten dollars, Ham4Ham was a catchy way of telling the audience members how much they could expect to pay if they won the lottery.

At the lotteries, such huge crowds would gather in front of the Richard Rodgers Theatre that Lin, members of the *Hamilton* cast, and guest stars began doing special performances just for the large group of people waiting on the street.

The show officially opened on August 6, 2015. The original Broadway cast included Lin as Alexander Hamilton, Daveed Diggs as Marquis de Lafayette and Thomas Jefferson, Renée Elise Goldsberry as Angelica Schuyler, and Phillipa Soo as Eliza Hamilton.

More than a month after *Hamilton*'s opening on Broadway, Lin was awarded a MacArthur Genius Grant. The grant is awarded to support creatives who've shown great potential so they can continue pursuing their passions. In his fellowship interview, Lin had emphasized, "This is a story about America then, told by America now," referring to the diversity of the cast and the use of hip-hop to present the United States' revolutionary history.

Among the earliest fans of the play was First
Lady Michelle Obama, who saw the show both
on and off-Broadway. Years after Lin's visit to the
White House, the First Lady became one of the
show's biggest supporters. On March 14, 2016,
she and President Obama showed their support
by hosting Lin once again, this time alongside his
cast, in an event entitled #Bam4Ham, meaning
"Obama for *Hamilton*."

At the #Bam4Ham event, the Obamas invited the *Hamilton* cast to perform songs from the play including "Alexander Hamilton," the song Lin had debuted seven years earlier; "My Shot"; "The Schuyler Sisters"; and "One Last Time." Bam4Ham also included an event where students got the chance to ask Lin and the rest of the cast questions.

On June 12, 2016, *Hamilton* was introduced

by the Obamas at the seventieth annual Tony Awards held at the Beacon Theatre in New York City. There, the First Lady referred to the show as "a musical about the miracle that is America." Lin's beach read had transformed from a single song to a Best Musical nominee with a record sixteen nominations, the most of any show in Tony history. Lin was nominated for Best Actor in a Musical, Best Original Score, and Best Book of a Musical. By the end of the night, *Hamilton* would go on to win eleven Tonys, including Best Score and Best Book for Lin and the biggest prize of all, Best Musical. Just under a month after the Tony Awards, Lin stepped down from his starring role as Alexander Hamilton.

While *Hamilton* connected Lin with the Obamas again, he also used his growing influence to voice his concerns about Puerto Rico in 2016. By that time, the island had been struggling with their finances for years, and the local government wanted to declare bankruptcy. When a person, place, or company declares bankruptcy, it means they admit they cannot pay off their debts and are asking for help. In Puerto Rico's case, most of the debt was owed to investors from the United States who took advantage of some of the financial decisions made by the local government.

By 2016, the United States' federal government was working on a law called the Puerto Rico Oversight, Management, and Economic Stability Act, or PROMESA. This law gave a board of representatives chosen by the president of the United States power over Puerto Rico's finances. Lin showed support for the proposal in articles he wrote for the *New York Times* and New York

City's first Spanish newspaper, *El Diario*. He also did a performance on John Oliver's *Last Week Tonight* where he asked representatives in Congress to show their support for Puerto Rico.

Lin understood that there were issues with the idea of Puerto Ricans having  no control over the board but wrote that it was the only action Congress was willing to take. By the end of June, Congress passed PROMESA and President Obama signed the law. This legislation established a financial management board for Puerto Rico.

In November 2016, Disney's *Moana* finally opened in movie theaters. Prior to its release, the movie earned strong reviews and became the second biggest Thanksgiving opening weekend ever at the time. Part of *Moana*'s success came from its

soundtrack, which families around the world loved. Lin contributed to a few songs for the movie, including the popular "You're Welcome," sung by Dwayne Johnson as Maui, and the beloved "How Far I'll Go," sung by Auli'i Cravalho as Moana. The magical movie about a Polynesian princess and a demigod was a hit, earning praise from critics and audiences alike.

CHAPTER 4
Beyond the Stage

At the February 2017 Academy Awards, *Moana* was nominated for Best Animated Feature Film and Lin was nominated for Best Original Song for "How Far I'll Go." At the awards show, Lin and the star of *Moana*, Auli'i Cravalho, provided a stunning performance of "How Far

I'll Go," highlighting Lin's writing ability and Auli'i's vocals. But Lin did not take home the award for Best Original Song.

Compared to the pace of the early 2010s, 2017 was a slow period for Lin. For the first half of the year, he was filming his role as Jack in Disney's *Mary Poppins Returns*, which starred Emily Blunt as the title character. Unfortunately, 2017 was anything but quiet for the island of Lin's heritage, Puerto Rico.

Hurricane María

On September 20, 2017, Hurricane María made landfall in Puerto Rico as a strong Category 4 storm. The island had already been suffering from the effects of a previous hurricane that season, which left many people without clean water and electricity. María worsened these issues, uprooting trees, damaging cell phone towers, and leaving all of Puerto Rico without power.

PUERTO RICO

WEATHER 9:50AM **HURRICANE MARÍA**

After Hurricane María, the United States, and particularly President Donald J. Trump's administration, faced criticism for their handling of the crisis. In the aftermath of the storm, it was hard for local Puerto Ricans to find and store food and clean water. The Federal Emergency Management Agency (FEMA) lost track of millions of dollars in supplies for the island.

By the end of 2017, the death toll remained unclear with only sixty-four deaths being counted by the government before the total was updated to 2,975 in August 2018. But other estimates put the actual number of casualties at around 4,645. The hurricane also caused about $90 billion in damages and is the deadliest storm in Puerto Rico's history.

Within a few weeks of Hurricane María making landfall in Puerto Rico, Lin and his father organized a group of Puerto Rican and other Hispanic-Latine artists to create a song entitled "Almost Like Praying." The money earned from the song was donated to the Hispanic Federation's fund for Hurricane María relief.

The song included Puerto Rican artists Marc Anthony, Rita Moreno, Gilberto Santa Rosa, Jennifer Lopez, and Fat Joe along with other Latine singers including Camila Cabello, Juan

Luis Guerra, and Rubén Blades. Altogether, the Hispanic Federation raised $14 million for Puerto Rico's relief and recovery efforts less than a month after the hurricane.

Beyond "Almost Like Praying," on November 8, 2017, Lin and Jeffrey Seller announced they would be bringing a fully staged production of *Hamilton* to Puerto Rico in January 2019 at the University of Puerto Rico's Teatro UPR.

Lin also shared that he would return to play the role of Alexander Hamilton for the show's limited run. His goal in bringing *Hamilton* to the island was to encourage tourism and raise money for local artists. While Puerto Rico wrestled with its recovery, Lin looked to help in the best way he knew, by performing.

At the end of 2017, Lin and Vanessa Nadal announced they were expecting another child. On February 2, 2018, Francisco Miranda, their second son, was born. Lin celebrated Francisco's birth with a tweet like the one he had shared for

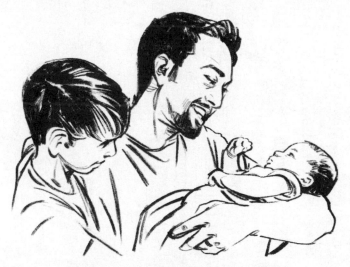

the birth of Sebastian, ending the post with the word "Intermission," meaning "a short break." But there seemed to be no break in sight for Lin!

Amid preparations for *Hamilton* in Puerto Rico, on July 22, 2018, the Mirandas, the *Hamilton* team, and the Flamboyan Foundation, a nonprofit organization based in Puerto Rico and Washington, DC, announced that they would be launching the Flamboyan Arts Fund.

FLAMBOYAN
ARTS FUND

LIN-MANUEL MIRANDA IS BACK AS
ALEXANDER HAMILTON TO SUPPORT
ARTS IN PUERTO RICO

The fund aimed to support arts organizations in Puerto Rico as the island and its residents recovered. In their announcement, the Flamboyan

Foundation shared that all profits from *Hamilton*'s time in Puerto Rico would be donated to the fund. Additionally, to ensure that the show could be seen by a wider audience, 9,600 tickets were going to be sold for ten dollars each under another lottery system. Lin's dad, Luis, worked with the *Hamilton* team to make the event a success. Luis had graduated from the University of Puerto Rico, so part of Lin's hope in bringing the show to the island was to honor his father.

In the weeks leading up to *Hamilton*'s debut in Puerto Rico, faculty members from the University of Puerto Rico, where the performance would be staged, indicated they would strike during the show. The faculty members were protesting budget cuts that had been made to the university. After talking with the *Hamilton* team, the strikers changed their minds, agreeing not to strike during *Hamilton*'s run. But, by then, the production had been moved to the Centro de Bellas Artes Luis A. Ferré Theatre.

The possibility of a strike was not the only controversy in bringing the live *Hamilton* show to Puerto Rico. Some students pointed out that *Hamilton* did not provide many paid opportunities for the local citizens of the island. Some felt that although the Flamboyan Arts Fund brought money to the arts in Puerto Rico, it did not address the larger—and perhaps more serious—hurricane reconstruction efforts.

There were also Puerto Ricans who were hurt by Lin's previous support for PROMESA. By then, the board that came as part of the law had caused budget cuts on the island that reduced funding for schools and healthcare while

bringing in more wealthy investors. Those investors would often buy property on the island and try to change it without any consideration for Puerto Rico's lifelong residents. Students showed their frustrations with Lin through protests and conversations on social media.

Ultimately, *Hamilton* played for thousands of people in Puerto Rico, with many local residents of the island receiving the ten-dollar tickets.

At the end of the first performance, Lin, dressed as Hamilton, shared, "a lot of people moved a lot of mountains to have us be here in Puerto Rico tonight and to raise as much money as we can for Puerto Rico while we're here." Then, he pulled a Puerto Rican flag from his Hamilton costume and waved it for the crowd.

After *Hamilton* completed its time in Puerto Rico, Lin and members of his Freestyle Love Supreme group brought their show to the Broadway stage for the first time. Each night, the rotating cast of the group would take word

suggestions from the audience and use them in new freestyle raps, showing off their quick thinking. This version of their show ran from October 2019 to January 2020. But, by March of 2020, much of our world had turned upside down.

CHAPTER 5
The Next Act

When 2020 lockdown orders caused by the COVID-19 pandemic began, live theater performances and movie sets were put on hold.

In their place, more streaming services emerged. One of Lin's projects that made its streaming debut that June was *We Are Freestyle Love Supreme*, a documentary film exploring the group's start through early video of their performances. At the heart of the documentary, just like the group itself, are a bunch of friends who love performing together. As Lin's collaborator

Thomas Kail shared, "it's probably the purest expression of joy that any of us have ever felt in doing a show."

Of course, Lin isn't just a writer, performer, and musician. He's also a dad! During the COVID-19 pandemic, most schools were not able to open classrooms for students. Since Lin and Vanessa were at home in Inwood, New York, for much of the time with their kids, Sebastian and Francisco, they did their best to help teach their sons. Francisco was only two years old in 2020 so he wasn't in school yet, but Sebastian was already in the first grade. Since Francisco saw his older brother working so hard at home, he decided to get to work, too. While Sebastian did his homework, Francisco started writing letters and practicing his numbers even at such a young age! Because of the extra time they were spending together, the two brothers became super close.

Sebastian and Francisco also showed a creative side during the pandemic. According to Lin, the boys began making up songs, especially about breakfast.

Sebastian also began making fun short films, often starring in them with Francisco while Lin recorded. Even though Lin had worked on a few movies himself, Sebastian wasn't starstruck by his dad's success. For the world, Lin may have been a genius, playwright, and important entertainer, but to Sebastian, he was still just his dad. The COVID-19 pandemic caused many challenges, but the Miranda family found ways to come together and have fun.

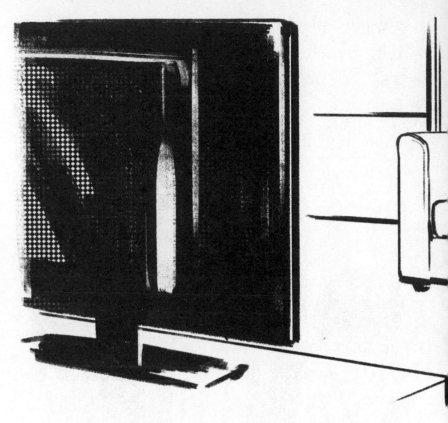

Originally, a film adaptation of *In the Heights* was scheduled to be released in theaters that June. But, because of the pandemic, it was pushed to 2021. Instead, the next project in Lin's schedule was the release of the recorded *Hamilton* show on the Fourth of July weekend. It featured all the

original Broadway cast members. By allowing
people to stream the stage production of *Hamilton*
at home, Lin and the *Hamilton* team were opening
the play to millions of people around the world at
an affordable price.

In the Heights was one of the first movies

to be released in theaters as the COVID-19 pandemic slowed for a period in June 2021. While writing the film, Lin reunited with Quiara Alegría-Hudes, his cowriter on the original play.

The film was directed by Jon M. Chu, best known for his 2018 adaptation of the novel *Crazy Rich Asians*. Although Chu was not Latine or from New York City, he saw pieces of his family's stories in *In the Heights*'s focus on the migrant experience and theme of finding a new home.

In the film, Lin put on a fake beard and took on the role of the *piragüero* behind the piragua cart. The film also starred Anthony Ramos as Usnavi, Melissa Barrera as Vanessa, Leslie Grace as Nina, and Corey Hawkins as Benny.

The movie version of *In the Heights* did receive some criticism online. Washington Heights, known in New York City as "Little Dominican Republic," is a largely Afro-Dominican neighborhood, and the lead cast of the film did not reflect the neighborhood's true population.

Instead of celebrating a broad view of *Latinidad* (Latine identity), critics felt the movie was erasing specific struggles faced by dark-skinned Latines, and continuing a pattern of colorism that exists throughout Latin America.

Colorism is a form of prejudice that treats people with darker skin worse than those with lighter skin and is a struggle for many ethnic groups, including Black and Asian communities.

In Latine communities, the colorism faced by darker-skinned people often means they are ignored in media like television, film, and music. Four days after the *In the Heights* film debuted, Lin posted a note on social media sharing that he was dedicated to learning and growing while trying to honor his diverse community.

Lin's next project was an animated film called *Vivo* about a Cuban kinkajou—a type of rainforest mammal. Lin starred as the voice of Vivo and wrote songs for the movie. In the film's

story, Vivo's friend, Andrés, dies before he can play a song for his true love, Marta. After the funeral, Vivo goes on a mission to give the song to Marta with help from Andrés's relative, Gabi.

Gabi is an outsider in her town because she prefers her independence over fitting into others' expectations.

Lin ended 2021 with a double feature. In November, the film adaptation of Jonathan Larson's *tick, tick . . . Boom!* was released. At forty-one years old, it was Lin's first time

working as a movie director. A couple of weeks later, the animated movie *Encanto* opened. This project, set in Colombia, tells a colorful story about the Madrigal family and the magical gifts they use to help their small town. The film's lead character, Mirabel Madrigal, doesn't have powers, but the rest of her family does. Mirabel struggles with feeling like her family is better than her because of their abilities. Ultimately, Mirabel helps her family see that it's their love that's the real miracle. Lin had written all the music for the movie. The soundtrack for *Encanto* was so popular that all eight of the songs Lin wrote made it onto *Billboard*'s Hot 100 chart at the same time.

(The Hot 100 counts the hundred most popular songs in the United States.) The full movie soundtrack also spent nine weeks at the top of *Billboard*'s Top 200 album chart, meaning it was the most popular album in the United States for that period.

The most popular song from *Encanto* centered on Mirabel's mysterious uncle, Tío Bruno, who could see the future but disappeared after being blamed for incidents he predicted.

For over a month, "We Don't Talk About Bruno" was the biggest song in the United States. It was the second from a Disney animated film to top the *Billboard* Hot 100 and had the longest run of any song from a Disney film soundtrack *ever*. "We Don't Talk About Bruno" became Lin's first song to top the

Hot 100. During that time, everyone was talking about Bruno! In fact, by the time *Encanto* was released, many schools had started reopening from the COVID-19 pandemic, and Sebastian Miranda's classmates were singing about Bruno, too!

Encanto featured a powerful cast of actors, mostly of Colombian descent. At the lead was Stephanie Beatriz as Mirabel Madrigal. She had previously worked with Lin in the 2021 version of *In the Heights*. Beatriz

Stephanie Beatriz

was joined by Jessica Darrow as Luisa, Diane Guerrero as Isabela, María Cecilia Botero as Abuela Alma, and John Leguizamo as Tío Bruno.

John Leguizamo

The popularity of *Encanto*'s soundtrack and representation of the Colombian Madrigal family made it a huge hit.

Both *tick, tick . . . Boom!* and *Encanto* received nominations at the March 2022 Academy Awards. *Tick, tick . . . Boom!* was nominated for

Best Actor in a Leading Role and also Best Film Editing. Meanwhile, *Encanto* was nominated for Best Animated Feature Film, Best Original Score, and Best Original Song for "Dos Oruguitas" ("Two Caterpillars"). Ultimately, *Encanto* won Best Animated Feature for 2022.

Cast of *tick, tick . . . Boom!* at the movie premiere, 2021

Also in 2022, Lin released a songbook (a book of lyrics and music) that collected songs from *In the Heights*, *Bring It On*, *21 Chump Street*, *Hamilton*, *Moana*, *Vivo*, and *Encanto*. He also contributed music to the Broadway play *New York, New York* and the live-action remake of *The Little Mermaid*. And in 2023, he appeared as Hermes in the television adaptation of *Percy Jackson and the Olympians*.

In recent decades, few people have had as big an impact on the entertainment industry and pop culture in general as Lin-Manuel Miranda has. He grew from being a high-energy young boy in Inwood to a rising star who wrote an award-winning play about his community. He's been to the White House (twice), risen to the top of the *Billboard* charts, starred on Broadway stages, and created big and small screen successes around the world. He has stayed true to his roots by still living just a mile away from his childhood home in Inwood with his wife, Vanessa, and two sons, Sebastian and Francisco. Today, Lin remains one of the most popular forces in entertainment as a valued songwriter, singer, actor, and creator.

102

Lin helped inspire a generation of musical theater fans, both on and off the stage. His legacy of catchy songs, huge films, and musical theater stardom go beyond what he could've imagined at his first piano recital. Still, just like back then, we're sure Lin will step back into the spotlight and remind us all that he "knows another one!"

Timeline of Lin-Manuel Miranda's Life

1980	Lin-Manuel Miranda is born in New York City on January 16
1998	Attends Wesleyan University where he eventually begins writing *In the Heights*
2003	Cofounds rap group Freestyle Love Supreme
2007	*In the Heights* opens off-Broadway on February 8
2008	*In the Heights* begins Broadway run
2009	Announces at the White House that he is working on a project called *The Hamilton Mixtape*
2010	Marries Vanessa Nadal on September 5
2014	Changes the name of *The Hamilton Mixtape* to *Hamilton*
	First son, Sebastian, is born
2015	*Hamilton* opens on Broadway on February 17
2016	Returns to White House to perform with *Hamilton* cast
	Disney film *Moana* debuts in theaters
2017	Plays Jack in *Mary Poppins Returns*
2018	Second son, Francisco, is born
2021	*In the Heights* film debuts on June 10
	Makes his directorial debut with the movie *tick, tick . . . Boom!*
	Disney film *Encanto* is released
2022	*The Lin-Manuel Miranda Collection* songbook is published

Timeline of the World

1980 — Ronald Reagan elected fortieth president of the United States

1981 — Prince Charles and Lady Diana Spencer marry in Great Britain on July 29

1983 — Microsoft releases the Microsoft Word computer program

1989 — In Germany, the Berlin Wall is torn down, leading to the end of the Cold War

1990 — Nelson Mandela is freed from prison in South Africa

2005 — Hurricane Katrina hits the United States in August, severely damaging Alabama, Louisiana, and Mississippi

2009 — Michael Jackson dies in Los Angeles, California, on June 25

2014 — Malala Yousafzai wins Nobel Peace Prize on October 10 for her activism, with the belief that every child has the right to an education

2015 — Same-sex marriage is recognized as a constitutional right by the US Supreme Court

2016 — *Pokémon GO* breaks records upon its release for most downloads in a single week on Apple app store

2020 — COVID-19 is declared a global pandemic by the World Health Organization

2022 — World population reaches over eight billion people

Bibliography

*Books for young readers

*Berrios, Frank. *The Story of Lin-Manuel Miranda: A Biography Book for New Readers*. Oakland, California: Rockridge Press, 2022.

*Calkhoven, Laurie. *You Should Meet: Lin-Manuel Miranda*. New York: Simon Spotlight, 2018.

Davis, Clayton. "Lin-Manuel Miranda Talks Jonathan Larson's Story in 'Tick, Tick . . . Boom!': 'It's about Failure.'" Variety Media LLC., *Variety*, Dec. 2, 2021, https://variety.com/2021/film/directors/Lin-miranda-songwriting-tick-tick-boom-encanto-in-the-heights-1235124156/.

The Obama White House. "Lin-Manuel Miranda Performs at the White House Poetry Jam: (8 of 8)." Nov. 2, 2009, YouTube video, https://youtu.be/WNFf7nMIGnE.

Ordoña, Michael. "Lin-Manuel Miranda Breaks Down the Success of 'We Don't Talk About Bruno' (No, No, No)." *Los Angeles Times*, March 8, 2022, https://www.latimes.com/entertainment-arts/awards/story/2022-03-08/lin-manuel-miranda-on-the-success-of-encanto-and-that-bruno-song.

Paulson, Michael. "Lin-Manuel Miranda, Creator and Star of 'Hamilton,' Grew up on Hip-Hop and Show Tunes." *New York Times*, Aug. 12, 2015, https://www.nytimes.com/2015/08/16/theater/lin-manuel-miranda-creator-and-star-of-hamilton-grew-up-on-hip-hop-and-show-tunes.html.

Pucl, Carlito. " 'In the Heights'—2008 Tony Awards—Best Original Score." June 16, 2008, YouTube video, 3:10, https://www.youtube.com/watch?v=ozuEXtuM1RM.

YOUR HEADQUARTERS FOR HISTORY

Activities, Mad Libs, and sidesplitting jokes!
Discover the Who HQ books beyond the biographies

Who? What? Where?

Learn more at whohq.com!

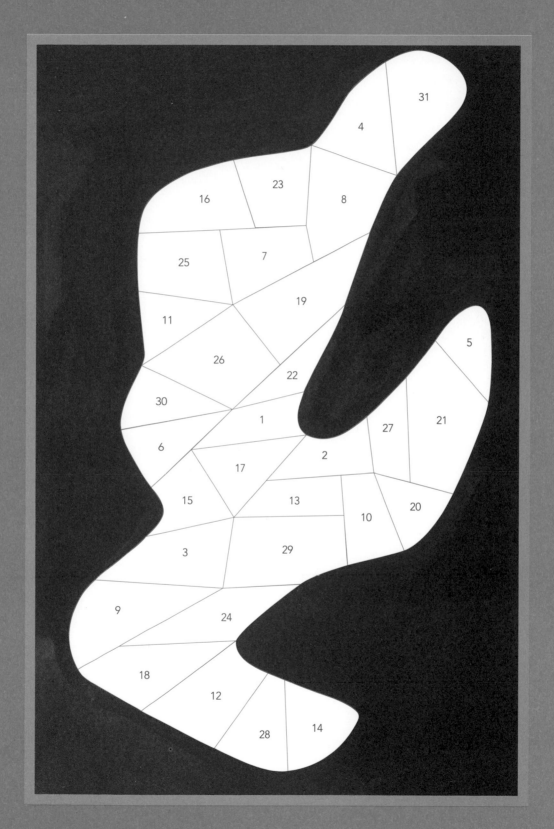

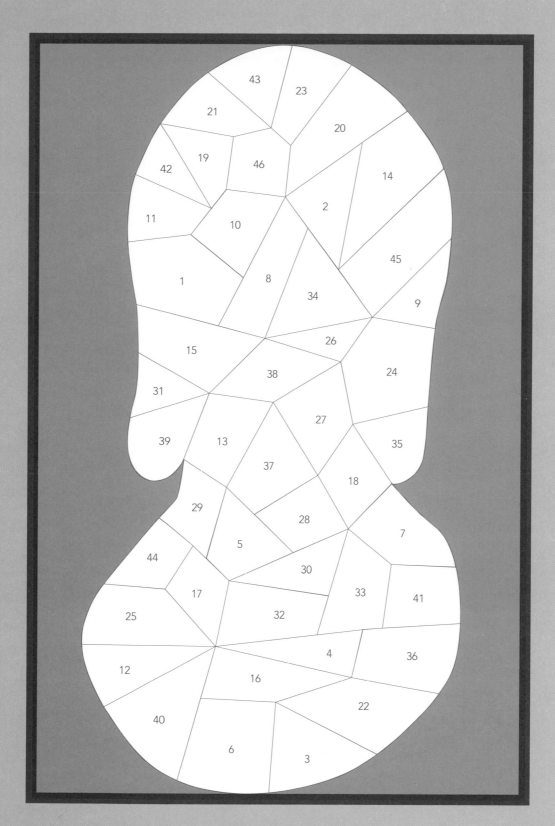

NINA SIMONE

OPRAH WINFREY

RUBY BRIDGES

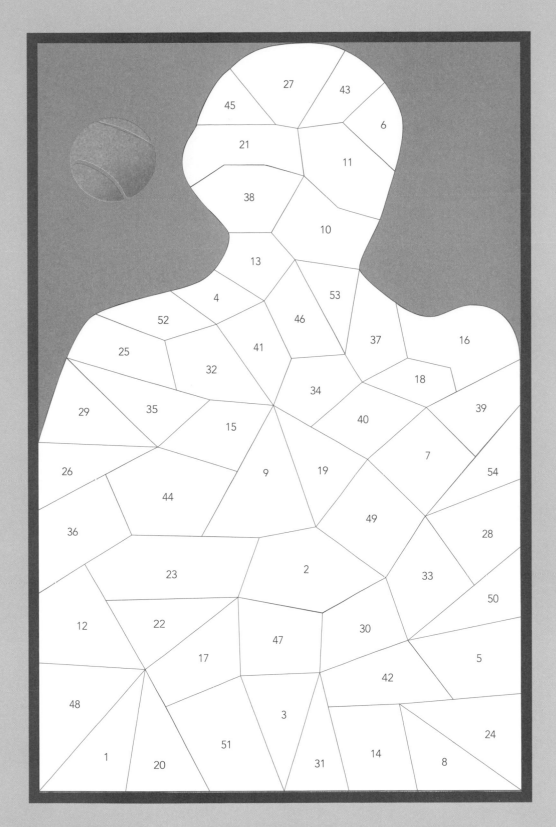

SERENA AND VENUS WILLIAMS

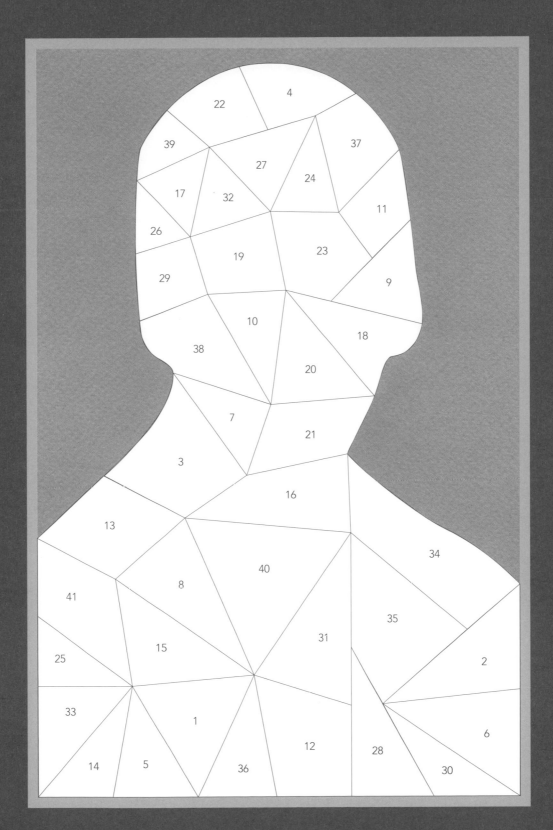

SOJOURNER TRUTH

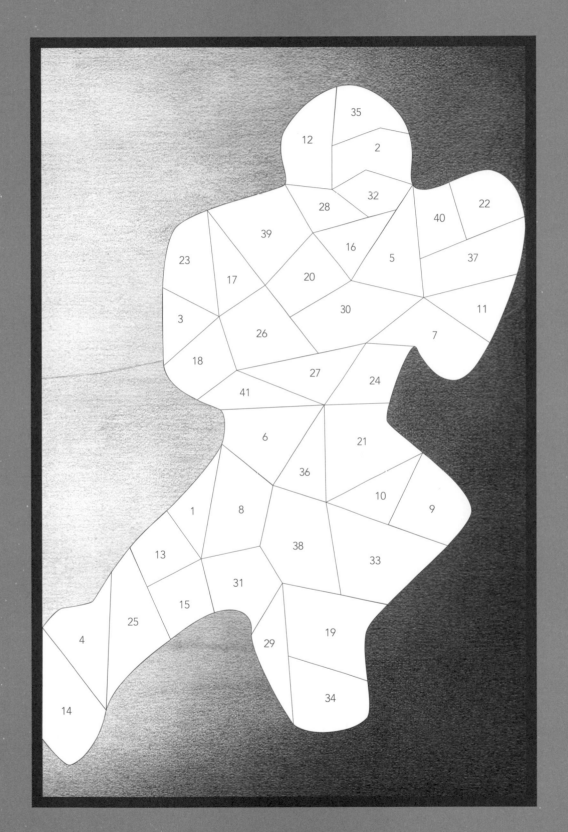

WILMA RUDOLPH

MADAM C. J. WALKER

HARRIET TUBMAN

IDA B. WELLS

KAMALA HARRIS

KATHERINE JOHNSON, DOROTHY VAUGHAN, AND MARY JACKSON

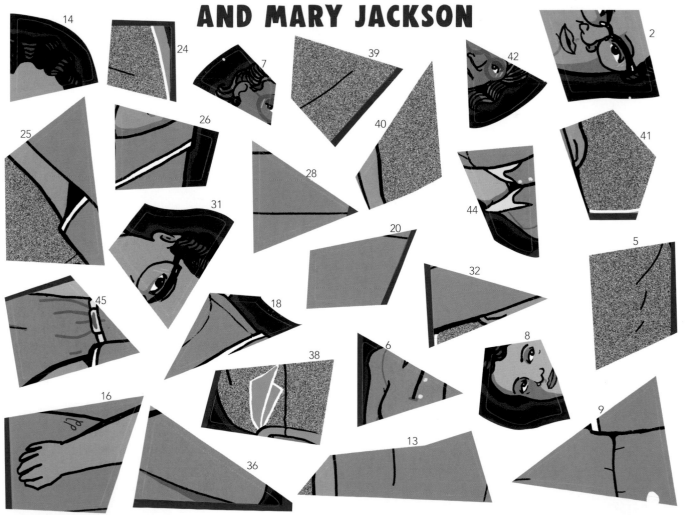

MISTY COPELAND

NINA SIMONE

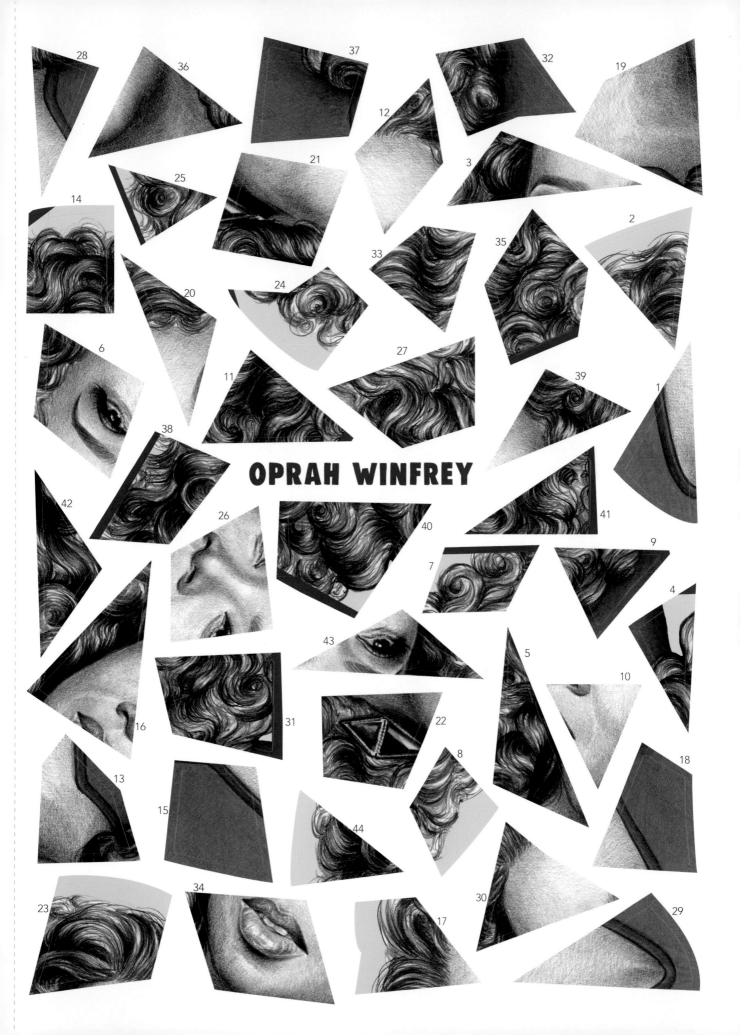

OPRAH WINFREY

RUBY BRIDGES

SERENA AND VENUS WILLIAMS

SOJOURNER TRUTH

WILMA RUDOLPH